Colorful Cities, LLC
1329 N 47th Street #31664
Seattle WA 98103
www.colorfulcities.com | info@colorfulcities.com

100% designed, illustrated and printed in the United States of America.

ISBN: 978-0-9898972-4-2
Library of Congress Control Number: 2019915742

Concept, Design & Text: Laura Lahm
Illustrations: Retsu Takahashi
Art Direction: Jenna Ashley
Cover Coloring: Julie Knutson

For more cities in the Explore & Color series please visit colorfulcities.com

A few great ways to *Explore & Color* Chicago, whether you're in the city or at home!

- Page Roulette! Turn to a random page and let that be your starting point to explore or color.

- See if you can visit all the locations using the L Train or your feet.

- Create a scavenger hunt based on the illustrations.

- Drop your pencil on the map and explore the nearest location to your landing point or color that illustration.

- Create a contest to explore as many of Colorful Chicago's locations as possible.

- Color an illustration then explore its history in more depth.

- See if you can pick out the UNESCO World Heritage Site captured in the book.

- Use these pages as art for your walls. Perforations at the top of the pages make this easy to do.

- If you are in Chicago, use the map and index to plan an itinerary based upon your favorite illustrations.

Are we missing a location in Chicago? Use the designated page at the end of the book to draw your favorite place to explore and don't forget to add it to the map. Share your drawing with us: hello@colorfulcities.com. We'd love to hear from you!

Are you ready to explore Chicago?

580 public parks and more than 8,000 acres of green space, 700 public art works, 56 amazing museums, 18 miles of accessible lakefront trails with 24 beaches. Chicago has something for everyone with its 77 diverse neighborhoods, 225 music venues, 250 theaters and 8 major sports teams (Go Blackhawks!). And, it is all completely accessible via 146 L train stations and 28 city bus routes (with 10,768 bus stops) throughout the greater metropolis.

In the late 1770s by the shores of Lake Michigan, Jean Baptiste Point DuSable established the first settlement of Chicago. It officially became a city in 1837, and quickly grew to become the largest city in the American Midwest. Even the Great Chicago Fire of 1871 (we all remember Mrs. O'Leary and her cow!) didn't stop it from growing to a city of a million over the next 20 years and becoming the third largest in the United States. It has a rich—at times controversial—history filled with heroes, villains, architecture that astonishes with its height, and a river that runs in reverse.

Now home to nearly 2.7 million people, Chicago has long attracted waves of Americans and immigrants chasing the American Dream. Diverse people and cultures have merged into one shared Chicago community, but their uniqueness can still be found within their individual neighborhoods. With so many places to discover, where do you start? We have some ideas!

Grab your sneakers and colored pencils—here we go! Bike the Lakefront Trail to Lincoln Park Zoo to see the gorillas feeding in the morning, and continue further south on the trail in the afternoon to the Garden of the Phoenix in Jackson Park. Looking for a creative angle to the city? Stroll through Millennium Park to gaze at your whimsical reflection in the Cloud Gate, or as people like to call it, "The Bean." Watch kids splash as water shoots from the revolving digitized faces of the Crown Fountain. Pop into the Chicago Art Institute for an education on French Impressionism, then cross the street to snap a picture of yourself next to the starting sign for Route 66. Parks on your list? You're in luck: hop on the L train to the Lincoln Park neighborhood to play among the statues of Dorothy and the Tin Man in Oz Park or cruise to Clarendon Park to play bocce ball—spend as little or as much time as you want on these fun, free activities. If you're trying to find a bit of quiet in this bustling city, head to the 9th floor Winter Garden of the Harold Washington Library or venture out to Promontory Point for a tranquil picnic along the water.

All this exploring is bound to leave you hungry, and one of the benefits of such a culturally-rich city is its mouth-watering cuisine. Deep-dish pizza, the Puerto Rican jibarito (plantains instead of bread!), corned beef sandwich (try Manny's in the South Loop), dim sum, Mother-in-Law (tamale on a bun—don't ask, just eat), soul food, traditional Ukranian cabbage rolls, Korean BBQ, and do not forget the famous Chicago Dog.

Whether you call it Chi-Town, the Windy City, or the City of Big Shoulders, there is just so much to explore. We've included a few of our favorite places to use as starting points, but there are no stopping points for this fabulous city, or for you. We hope you wonder and wander beyond the pages of this book.

Happy Exploring and Welcome to Chicago!

——————————————— ☆ ☆ ☆ ☆ ———————————————

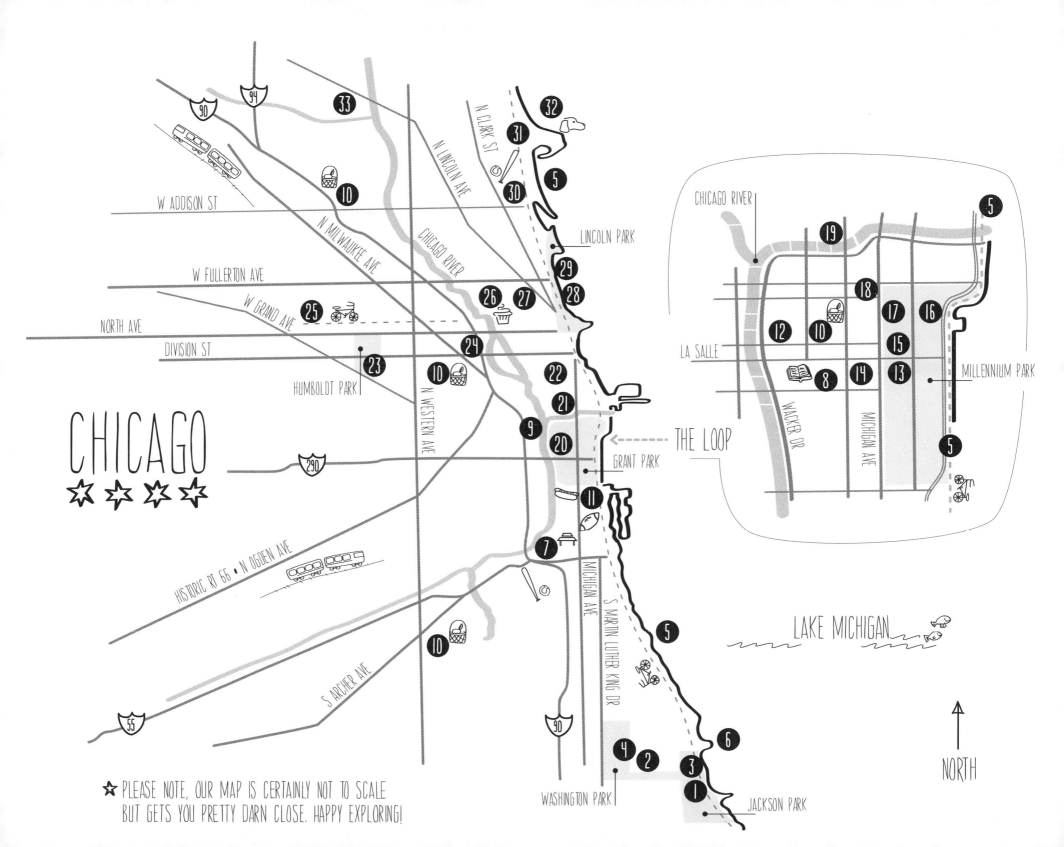

COLORFUL CHICAGO LOCATIONS

Please note the information was correct at the time of publication, but as with all things in life it is subject to change. Happy exploring!

An enduring reminder of Chicago's 160-year relationship with Japan, Jackson Park is home to the Japanese-inspired **Garden of the Phoenix**. The island garden, featuring the Phoenix Pavilion, was created for the 1893 Chicago World's Fair by Japanese representatives and has been recently restored. You'll find this serene park is a perfect place for a quiet stroll or afternoon picnic. • gardenofthephoenix.org

The Frederick C. **Robie House** is a national historic landmark and part of *The 20th Century Architecture of Frank Lloyd Wright* UNESCO World Heritage inscription. Located on the University of Chicago campus, it is one of the last houses designed by Frank Lloyd Wright in his Oak Park Studio. This 1910 home is considered the premier example of American Prairie-style architecture, with concepts significantly ahead of their time such as open floor plans, furniture designed specifically for the space, and the integration of interior and exterior space. Tours available. • flwright.org

With over 400,000 square feet of exhibition space, the **Museum of Science and Industry** is the largest science center in the Western Hemisphere. Discovery and curiosity are front and center in the museum's large array of interactive science exhibits. Diverse permanent exhibits include the art deco Pioneer Zephyr train from the 1930s; the U-505, a German submarine from WWII; and a baby chick hatchery. So much to explore! • msichicago.org

Rich in historic artifacts and artwork, the **DuSable Museum of African American History** is dedicated to the study and conservation of African American history, culture, and art. A variety of events, performances, and exhibits provide a creative platform for a deeper appreciation and telling of so many personal and societal events. Named for Jean Baptiste Point DuSable, who established the original trading post and settlement in 1779 that would eventually become Chicago. • dusablemuseum.org

"The Lakefront by right belongs to the people," wrote Daniel Burnham, Chicago urban designer, in 1909. And so it became. The **Lakefront Trail** is an 18-mile paved path letting pedestrians and bikers experience the beauty of Lake Michigan. It begins near the South Shore Cultural Center, passes through 13 neighborhoods (including downtown), and ends at Kathy Osterman Beach on the north end. • chicagoparkdistrict.com

For spectacular views of the Chicago skyline, you can't beat **Promontory Point**. Located just off the southern section of the Lakefront Trail, this is a perfect place for a tranquil picnic surrounded by water. Bike here in the summer months and enjoy swimming, windsurfing, and kayaking. • chicagoparkdistrict.com

Dumplings, dim sum, or duck? Such delightfully delicious decisions! Limitless menu options await you at a lunch date in **Chinatown**, just south of downtown. When you're done, go explore! You'll find herbalists, historical museums, a beautiful replica of Beijing's Nine-Dragon Wall and grocery stores with some of the biggest and smallest bowls you can imagine. If you are visiting in late winter, then be sure to check out the Lunar New Year celebration.

Despite its name, the **Winter Garden** on the 9th floor of Harold Washington Library Center is less a garden than a public reading and work space. But don't let this deter you! As you leave the elevators, you'll be dazzled by the natural light coming through the glass ceiling and surrounded by the art deco interior and tropical palms. Grab a book and enjoy this free, public space that's open year-round. • chipublib.org

The **L train**, short for elevated, is the Chicago Transit Authority's (CTA) elevated, underground, and street-level transit system. Over its 125-year existence, the L train has grown to over 140 stations, making Chicago easy to navigate and neighboring suburbs accessible. It's the easiest (and cheapest) way to reach either of the two main airports. See the city like a local! transitchicago.com

10 There are well over 20 city-sponsored **farmers markets** throughout Chicago, along with countless other local stands selling fresh produce from Midwestern farmers. Be sure to also enjoy artisans selling their wares - handmade soaps, steamed chicken tamales or gourmet dog biscuits. • chicago.gov

11 If you get hungry while exploring, then experience the culinary phenomenon created for the 1893 World's Fair—the **Chicago-style Hot Dog**. This low-cost street food consists of an all-beef hot dog, known as a "red-hot," on a poppy seed bun, topped with diced onions, tomato slices, dill pickles, sport peppers, celery salt, green relish, and yellow mustard. No ketchup please!

12 Step out on **The Ledge at the Skydeck Chicago** to experience one of the best views of the Chicago skyline and surrounding states beyond. From 1,353 feet above, visitors hover in glass boxes that extend 4.3 feet out from the Skydeck. They may wonder if it's the panorama or the height that has taken their breath away—they are on top of the Willis (formerly Sears) Tower, the tallest building of the Chicago skyline. • theskydeck.com

13 Whether you're a fan of Grant Wood's iconic "American Gothic" or prefer the tranquility of Claude Monet's "Water Lilies", **The Art Institute of Chicago** is your place. Its vast collection spans styles, continents, and mediums. The building is famous for its Beaux-Arts style of architecture as well as the two bronze lions that flank the main entrance. The Art Institute offers tours, education for children and adults, and an extensive architectural library. • artic.edu

14 Get your kicks on Route 66, the historic highway that spans from the Midwest all the way to the West Coast and has been inspiring road trips for generations. You'll find the Historic **Route 66 Begin** sign in downtown Chicago, battered and often covered with stickers. Look for it across the street from The Art Institute.

15 **Crown Fountain**, designed by Jaume Plensa, is an interactive (and potentially immersive!) public art feature in Chicago's Millennium Park. Two towers made up of LED screens overlook a granite pool and display the faces of 1,000 Chicagoans—with water spraying from their mouths! It's a novel, friendly integration of technology with community, and a great place to people-watch or to cool off with a splash in the water. • millenniumparkfoundation.org

16 Your expedition to Millennium Park wouldn't be complete without a trip across the bridge to the welcoming 20-acre **Maggie Daley Park**, designed to blend in with the pre-existing natural landscape. The highlight of your winter visit is the amazing skating ribbon with hot chocolate stops along the way. • maggiedaleypark.com

17 Better known as "The Bean" due to its unique shape, **Cloud Gate** attracts young and old to gaze at their whimsical reflections. Inspired by the appearance of liquid mercury, the sculpture is completely seamless, polished stainless steel. Designed by Anish Kapoor, Cloud Gate sits at the center of Millennium Park, with stunning views of Chicago's towering buildings behind and the sky above. • millenniumparkfoundation.org

18 The **Chicago Cultural Center** is a municipal venue offering music, theater, dance, and exhibitions devoted to the visual arts and contemporary culture. The rich architecture of the interior is truly lovely, but the magnificent Tiffany Dome—the world's largest of its kind—is the star, featuring the 12 zodiac signs and comprised of over 30,000 fish scale shaped pieces of glass. Tours of the building, affectionately named the "People's Palace", are available year-round and are free to the public. • chicagoculturalcenter.org

19 Chicago is known for its collection of moveable drawbridges that span the Chicago River. Otherwise known as bascule bridges, most are 70 to 100 years old and still function on their original counterbalance mechanisms. Designed to allow working ships to pass, now the bridges only open in spring and fall, primarily for sailboats on their way to and from Lake Michigan.

20 Chicago is home to four of the ten tallest buildings in the United States, making it one of the most towering and magnificent skylines. There's no shortage of places from which to enjoy the panorama, and you'll find that every perspective of the city's silhouette is truly one of a kind. Especially after you've been exploring on the ground, it's fun to get a bird's-eye view.

21 One of only a few buildings to survive the Great Chicago Fire, the **Chicago Water Tower** is a striking reminder of Chicago's industrial roots against a sea of modern skyscrapers. This treasured landmark currently serves as an art gallery and its surrounding walkways and benches are a convenient meeting spot. • watertowerarts.org

22 The **Newberry Library** is a free, independent research library housing a world-famous humanities collection. Accessible to the public since 1887, the building hosts not only citizen researchers, but also a number of exhibits and programs throughout the year. Visitors are welcome anytime to view the Newberry's galleries and learn about its collection. • newberry.org

23 The only museum in the nation focused on Puerto Rican art is located in the center of Humboldt Park, the heart of Chicago's Puerto Rican community. **The National Museum of Puerto Rican Arts & Culture** houses three galleries as well as spaces for art classes, exhibitions, and performances. The three paintings in the illustration are a part of "Expresión de Barrio" by Reynaldo Rodriguez. Admission to this wonderful gem is free! • nmprac.org

24 **Pulaski Park** was built in 1912 in an effort to expand neighborhood parks into Chicago's West Side. The park's main feature is its public fieldhouse and a large outdoor public pool surrounded by historic brownstone row houses. Throughout the year, Pulaski Park hosts special events, such as Movies in the Parks and holiday celebrations, which are free and open to the public. • chicagoparkdistrict.com

25 In the early 1990s, the City of Chicago proposed converting the abandoned Bloomingdale train line's elevated tracks into a pathway and green space. Thus became **The 606** (a reference to the local area code). This urban oasis, with great views of the city, serves as a pedestrian and bike route connecting a network of parks and northwest neighborhoods. • the606.org

26 A warm neighborly bakery in the heart of the Lincoln Park neighborhood, **Sweet Mandy B's** Old-Fashioned Desserts is famous for its pastel buttercream-topped cupcakes and delicious pastries, cakes, and other desserts. How about a confetti cookie or a red velvet cupcake? • sweetmandybs.com

27 **Oz Park** was created in 1976 in honor of The Wonderful Wizard of Oz author, L. Frank Baum, who resided nearby. Over the decades, sculptures of the Tin Man, Cowardly Lion, Scarecrow, and Dorothy & Toto have cropped up in this local "Oz." The park features Dorothy's Playlot, the Emerald Garden, tennis courts, and sports fields. • chicagoparkdistrict.com

28 A favorite weekend destination for Chicagoans, **Lincoln Park Zoo** is home to diverse wildlife, from an American black bear to dozens of Chilean flamingos, and expansive gardens filled with native plants. This 150-year-old zoo's mission is to provide meaningful experiences, connecting the people of Chicago with nature from around the world. The best part? The zoo is free year-round! • lpzoo.org

29 The **Lincoln Park Conservatory** is a step back in time to Chicago's industrial age. As smoke stacks and factories went up throughout the city, people became increasingly drawn to nature. Hence, the small greenhouse in Lincoln Park, aided by innovations in glass and steel architecture, became the grand conservatory that still exists today. One of our favorite botanical finds is the tropical sausage tree (Kigelia Africana), which hails from Africa but thrives in this lush greenhouse. The red blossoms only appear at night, and when pollinated, develop into long fruit looking like sausages! • lincolnparkconservancy.org

30 **Wrigley Field** was built in 1914 during the heyday of baseball. As host to the Chicago Cubs for over 100 years, it's the second oldest ballpark in the United States. Be sure to pay your respects to the statue of famed shortstop Ernie Banks, designed by Lou Cella. Grab a traditional Chicago-style hot dog as you settle in to enjoy a summer afternoon on the North Side of the city. • chicago.cubs.mlb.com

31 The bocce courts in the **Clarendon Community Center Park** are free and offer the neighborhood a relaxing environment to play this friendly, yet sometimes competitive, sport. chicagoparkdistrict.com

32 Chocolate lab, corgi, or husky - all canines are welcome at **Montrose Dog Beach** in the Uptown neighborhood of north Chicago. The MonDog organization is a non-profit that helps maintain this dedicated beach as a safe, off-leash space for dogs (and their people!) to play. • mondog.org

33 **River Park** is a quiet natural area located on the northern branch of the Chicago River, just as it splits into two. With just over 28 acres and a wildlife habitat, this park is the perfect place to explore the outdoors. How often do you get to jump into a kayak and paddle in the heart of the city? • chicagoparkdistrict.com

GARDEN OF THE PHOENIX

ROBIE HOUSE

MUSEUM OF SCIENCE AND INDUSTRY

DUSABLE MUSEUM OF AFRICAN AMERICAN HISTORY

LAKEFRONT TRAIL

PROMONTORY POINT

CHINATOWN

WINTER GARDEN

SWEET CORN
$50 EACH
$5.00 DOZEN

SNAP PEAS $3.00

HEIRLOOM TOMATOES $4.00/lb

Blueberries $3.00

$5.00 POUND

COLLARD GREENS $2.00 EA

ONIONS $3.00 BUNCH

Carrots $3.00 Bunch

TURNIP $2.00 POUND

PORTOBELLO $10.00 POUND

ZUCCHINI $2.00 POUND

SCALLIONS $1.00

WICKER PARK FARMERS MARKET

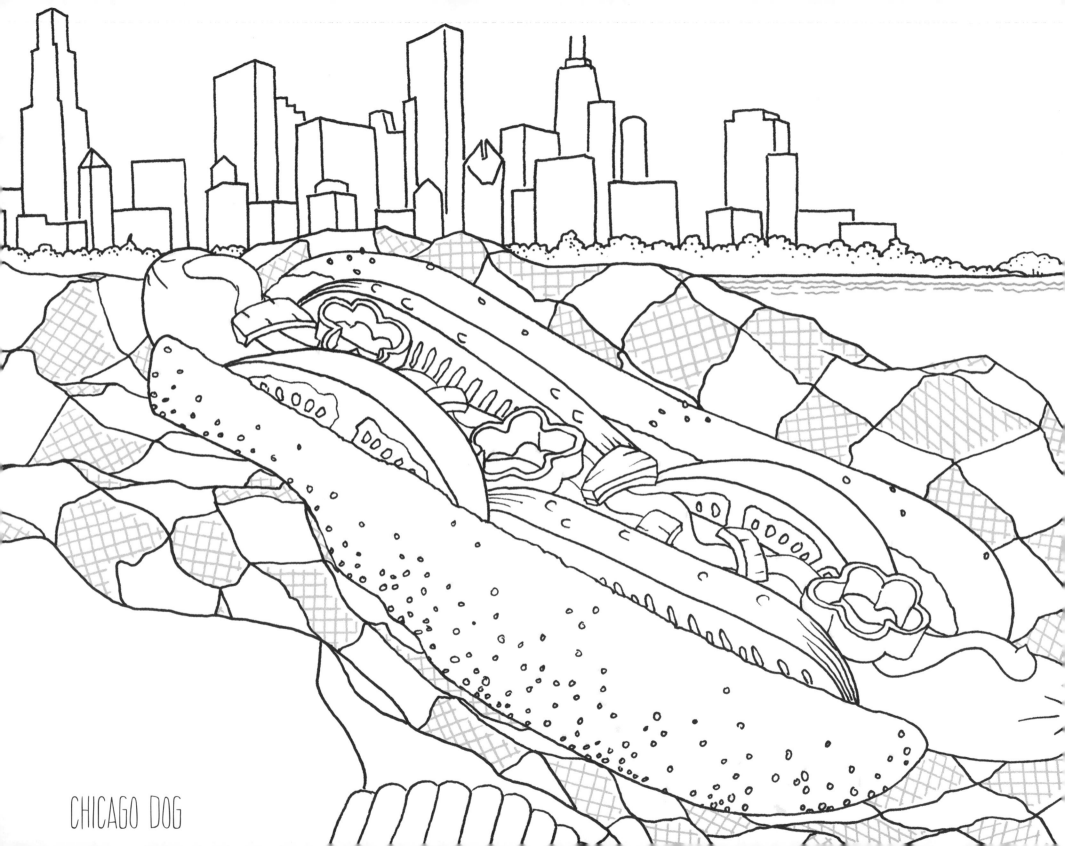

CHICAGO DOG

THE LEDGE AT SKYDECK CHICAGO

CROWN FOUNTAIN

MAGGIE DALEY PARK

CLOUD GATE

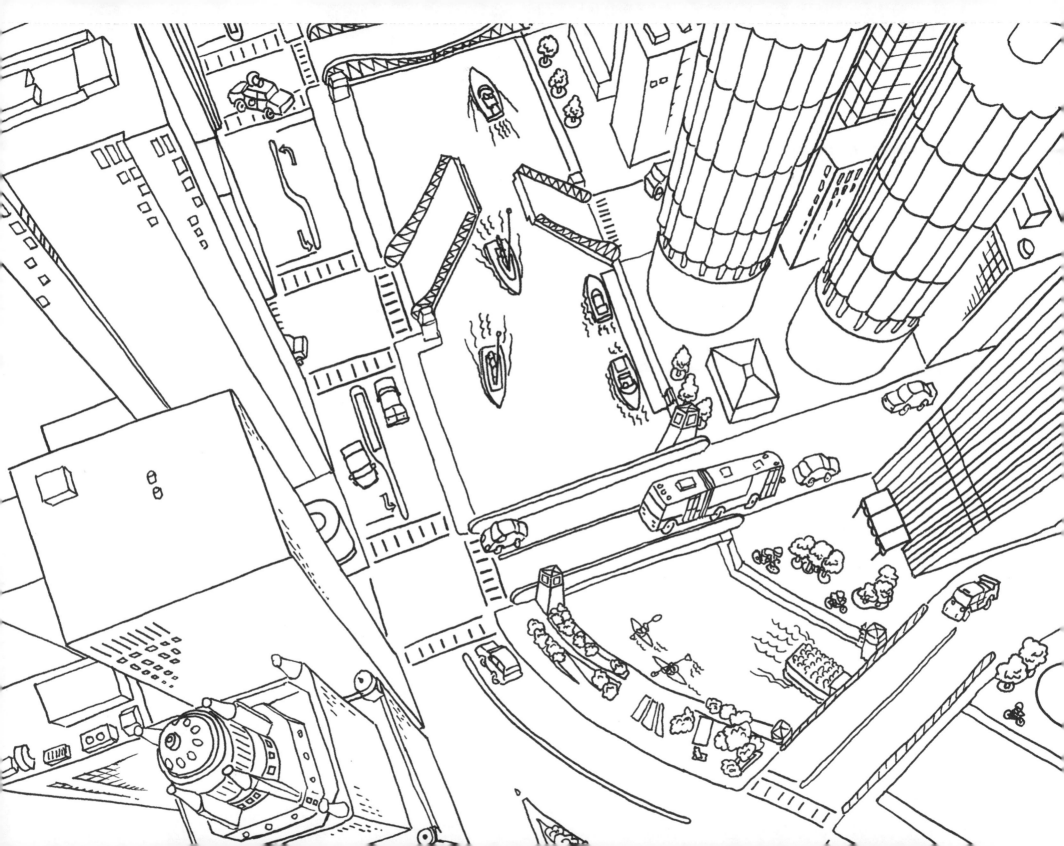

WATER TOWER

THE NEWBERRY

NATIONAL MUSEUM OF PUERTO RICAN ARTS & CULTURE

PULASKI PARK

THE 606

SWEET MANDY B'S

OZ PARK

LINCOLN PARK ZOO

LINCOLN PARK CONSERVATORY

CLARENDON BOCCE COURT

MONTROSE DOG BEACH

RIVER PARK

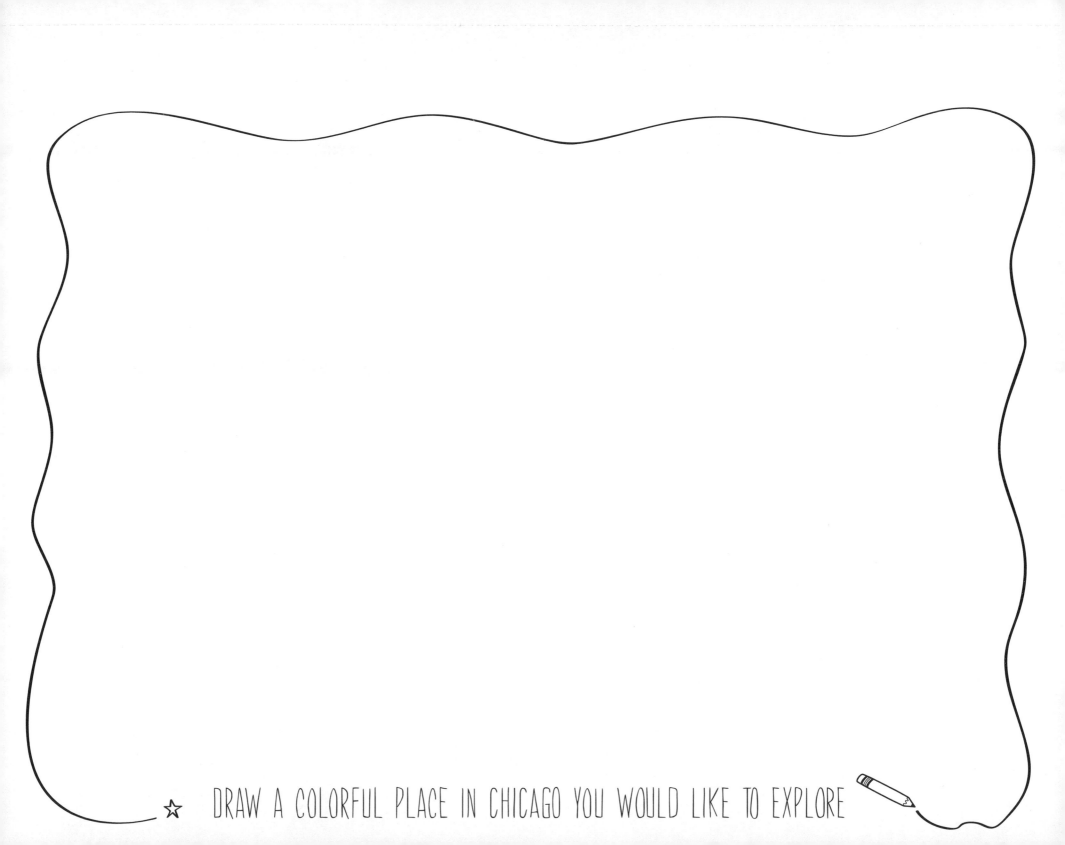

DRAW A COLORFUL PLACE IN CHICAGO YOU WOULD LIKE TO EXPLORE